“THI[illegible]

If you are confused when it comes to the debate [illegible] ion verses evolution, then this booklet is for you.

If you have doubted that there is a God and that He is in control, then this booklet is for you.

If you just like bugs, then this booklet is for you!

If you have never particularly liked those little “things that creepeth,” I can guarantee this booklet will change your mind.

I want you to come away from reading this booklet with a newly discovered knowledge of three things…

1. The **WISDOM** of God in His awesome creation.
2. The **WONDER** of God in this world.
3. The **WARNING** God gives us in nature.

Come with me and let’s look at
“Things that Creepeth…”
-Jeff Tichelar

"And God said, Let us make man in our image, after our likeness: and let them have dominion over the fish of the sea, and over the fowl of the air, and over the cattle, ***and over all the earth, and over every creeping thing that creepeth upon the earth.****"*
Genesis 1:26 (KJV)

When we look at the physical, tangible, observable universe, in particular when we look at this planet earth, do we see evidence of creation or evolution? Keep in mind that creation reveals God's invisible qualities, His eternal power and His divine nature. By contrast, evolution teaches that the world is the result of chance, chaos, order out of disorder, an accident or luck. So you will have to choose. You will have to do your own thinking, but I am going to show you some facts to help you decide.

75% of the animal kingdom is made up of insects!

If numbers were the measure of success, then beetles are the most successful animals on the face of the earth. When we look at the number of beetle species, a few comparisons will help us to get a grasp on the magnitude of this group. Keep in mind that there are 9,000 known bird species, and there are 4,000 known mammal species.

When I mention species, I am talking about those groups that are able to crossbreed. For example, there are many breeds of dogs, but they make up only one species. When you total up all the vertebrates, animals with backbones, all combined you will come up with 46,140 different species.

By contrast, more than 1 million insect species have been identified and cataloged.

You also need to note that there are approximately 5,000 to 10,000 new species of insects being discovered every year. Some believe that the total number of undiscovered insect species may be as high as 2 million. There is one scientist at the Smithsonian studying insects in the rain forest canopy. He believes the number is closer to 14 million undiscovered species. Some researchers estimate that the number may go as high as 30 million. It is absolutely fantastic!

This brings to mind that as our telescopes become more powerful and we look further and further into the universe, more and more stars are discovered. You cannot contain God – He just never runs out of wonderment. Have you noticed that? The same thing is true in the insect world.

One example of God's precision in the insect world is the mosquito. If you look at the mouthpart of the mosquito (the part that goes into your skin) under a microscope, it is perfectly sharp, straight and smooth! Man has attempted to copy this design when he created the hypodermic needle. But no matter how smooth and sharp we try to make them, if you look at a needle under a microscope, they are rough and jagged. Our Creator makes it difficult to deny His design.

The closer you look at the creations of men, the rougher and more inadequate they are. The closer you look at God's creation, the more intricate, perfect and wondrous it becomes!

Setting aside the insect species estimates and working with just the identifiable insects, the ratios are still awesome! Consider that 75% of the animal kingdom is made up of insects, 75% of those insects belong to one order, COLEOPTERA. COLEOPTERA is a Greek word meaning "sheath wing," "wing case" or "wing cover." It refers to the hard shell case that covers the wings. The wing case is made up of two halves and serves as the forward, fully functional wing set. These are the beetles. In other words, more than 50% of all animal species belong to one order, the beetles. So they are by far the absolute winners when it comes to sheer numbers.

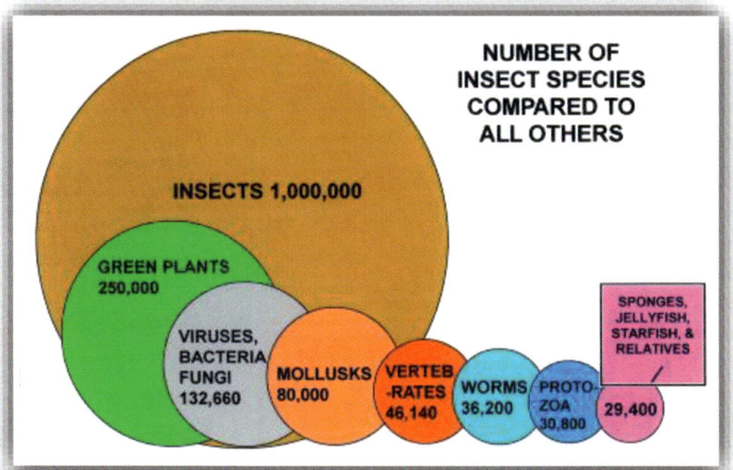

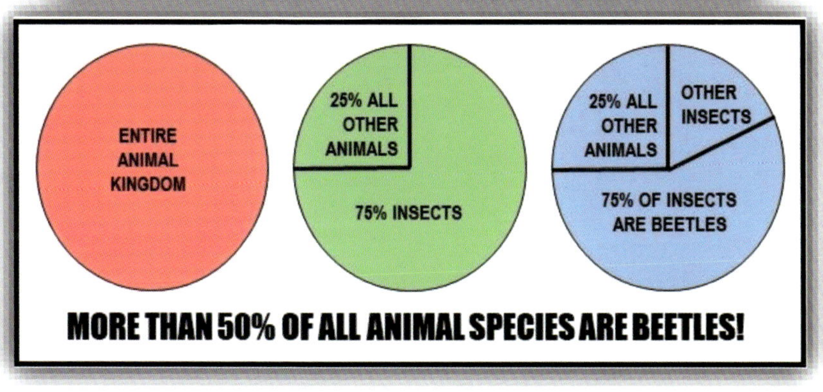

Now let's compare the creepers to man.

Did you know that there are 200 million insects for every single person on planet earth? Imagine 200 million insects! The weight of 200 million insects is 20,000 tons. In other words, there are 40 million pounds of bugs for every single one of us! Is that enough? If you do not like insects that might be a little distressing, but we need to understand that many of these insects are beneficial, not harmful! I'll show you just how beneficial a little further on.

Records held by beetles…

The largest insect is a beetle. Either the elephant beetle (MEGASOMA), or the granddaddy of them all, TITANUS-giganteus (a giant Cerambycid). This monster ranges in size from 10 to 16 centimeters, with the largest one on record reaching a whopping 20 centimeters! (That is nearly 8 inches of bug!) Note: In 2001, one specimen that was slightly over 16 centimeters was auctioned off for over three thousand dollars.

The smallest insect is also a beetle. Feather wing beetles are smaller than the period at the end of this sentence. They are so small they can fly through the eye of a needle, and for fun, wind surf on dust particles.

The record for the heaviest flying insect is held by the Goliath beetle.

Goliath Larva and Beetle

The strongest insect, also a beetle, is in the rhinoceros family of beetles and the surest footed, the leaf eating beetle.

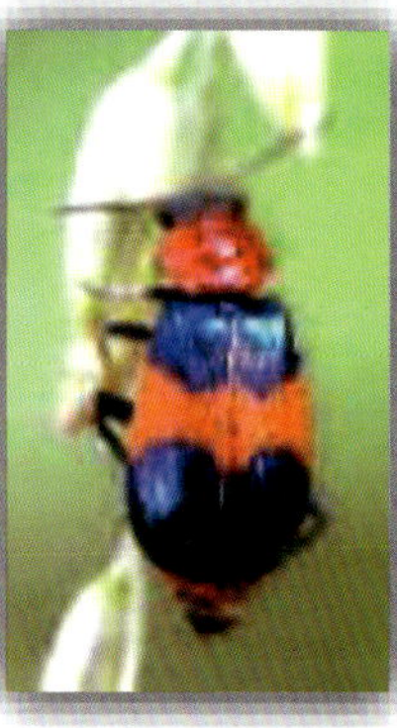

The insect group with the greatest number of secrets, mysteries, and the greatest number of questions that science cannot answer - you guessed it - the beetles!

The animals (not just restricted to insects) with the greatest responsibility of keeping this planet clean are the beetles!

Albert Einstein (not a Christian) said the following in a concluding address to the faculty of the California Institute of Technology:

"Gentlemen, the deeper I delve into the sciences of this Universe, the more firmly do I believe that ONE GOD, or FORCE, or INFLUENCE has ORGANIZED all of it for our DISCOVERY."

He saw order and symmetry that he referred to as* MATHEMATICAL ELEGANCE, *but he could never comprehend that a God so great could also be our personal God...

This was an individual who was a powerful figure, tremendously intelligent, a genius, who as far as I can tell, did not become a Christian. But when he looked at God's creation and saw the order and symmetry, he could see that someone arranged it and organized it to be discovered. Doesn't it sound like God? It does to me! God makes it difficult to deny His wisdom and power!

MEN ARE WITHOUT EXCUSE!

"For since the creation of the world God's invisible qualities—His eternal power and divine nature—have been clearly seen, being understood from what has been made, ***SO THAT MEN ARE WITHOUT EXCUSE.****"*
-Romans 1:20 (NIV)

God has clearly given us evidence of Himself in creation, so that we are without excuse to deny Him! Let's examine some of the evidence found among the beetles.

Eating habits of beetles...

I want to tell you about the eating habits of beetles. It is not hard to see why some people consider insects pesky in general, but if we learn a little more about them, we will thank God for them! The benefits of the beetles are greater than any ill effects. Remember also, that even the pesky ones provide food for many other animals.

Beetles could live very easily without man, but man could not live without beetles.

Beetles are herbivores, predators, parasites, and scavengers. As herbivores they feed on plant matter, as predators they prey on other animals, as parasites they live on or in other animals and as scavengers they feed on refuse and carrion.

Refuse refers to the dung droppings of other animals or some useless part of something that was once living. *Carrion* refers to dead and decaying flesh or carcasses. Beetles can consume a full range of plant tissue, whether it be living or decaying from underground roots to the leaves in the highest part of the rain forest canopy. They eat it all. They are a magnificent example of recycling. But, the beetle's greatest claim to fame in my personal opinion is that they are earth's "sanitation engineers."

God's primary way of keeping this planet clean and livable is the beetles.

There is no creature on earth that is more efficient, whether by physical or metabolic means for breaking down tons of organic material every day. They reduce it into material that plants will use as compost or animals will eat. There is a precise balance in this system.

Dung beetles have specially designed serrated feet and a head that is in the shape of a shovel. Each part is designed for its task. His front feet and head are designed so that he can dig and work with fecal material. Some of this material he will eat. Some he will form into a perfect ball so he can roll it to another site where the female lays her eggs and the dung ball will provide plenty of food. It is an amazing thing to understand how God has designed these little creatures to keep our planet clean!

Some dung beetles are called **generalists**. They are not fussy; they will eat the dung of any animal, but the one thing they will not do is eat old dung. It has to be fresh and it has to be of the right consistency. If the dung is on the ground too long and the sun hits it and starts to bake it, then it gets hard and loses its workability.

There are also other types of dung beetles. They are called **specialists**. The specialists are very fussy. They will only eat the dung of a specific animal. It is very interesting to consider some of the methods they have for sticking close to their favorite "source" of dung. One example is the beetle "Uroxys gorgon." It attaches to the fur of its favorite dung source, which happens to be the three-toed sloth. The three-toed sloth likes to be up high in the canopy of the rain forest, but comes down to relieve himself and guess who is along for the ride when he comes down? You guessed it - "Uroxys gorgon!" **He hangs onto the fur very close to the discharge point with specially designed claws, then at just the right moment, he grabs onto the emerging feast and rides it to the ground like a cowboy on a bucking bronco!** He doesn't waste any time.

Some dung beetles have antennas and sensing hairs so sensitive that they can detect the drop of a dung ball before it actually hits the ground.

That is absolutely amazing. They have such a sensitive detection system, that some can pick up the scent of dung a mile away and be there within minutes!

South African dung beetles are, I think, one of the most awesome examples of specialization and efficiency. They are flying around looking for zebra and elephant "pies." Their super sensitive antennas are out in the wind and pick up the aroma in less than a minute after the smell has become airborne. Keep in mind there are millions of dung beetles working the meadows and grasslands of Africa.

Also, keep in mind that there would be no grasslands if it were not for the beetles.

All of the animals that depend on grazing (the hoof stock) would die without dung beetles. All of the carnivores that eat the hoof stock would then also die. You would not have any of these animals if it were not for the beetles. Why? There is a misconception. Some think that all those droppings are good for the grasslands, but they are not. What happens when your neighbor's dog does his business on your front lawn? You end up with a burned spot that turns yellow and dies off. It is because of the high concentration of ammonia and digestive acids in that dropping. It is harmful until it has been composted. You are forced to go out and clean it up, so that it doesn't ruin your grass.

What needs to happen on the grasslands, so that it doesn't turn into one big sewer? Who is going to clean up after all those millions of animals? God uses the beetles! We could not live on this planet without these tiny janitors.

Accident or design?
God provided an awesome design in these wondrous little workers that go and clean up.

Do you have any idea how long it takes a swarm of dung beetles to clean up after a herd of 50 well-fed zebras? A million beetles will clean up the entire area **in less than**

three minutes. That is efficient! Remember it has to be fast because the sun dries the stuff out and they cannot work with it. The beetle eats what it can on the spot, and then without wasting anything carves the rest into a ball that it can roll away. It can either bury the ball on the spot or roll it to a better location.

To further see the importance of these beetles, let's look at just one species of hoof stock. It is estimated that the wildebeest produces 4,000 tons of dung every day in South Africa. That is 8 million pounds per day! Start calculating day after day and multiply that by all of the animals on all of the continents and then take away the dung beetles and you would have one huge toilet. God gave us a real gift in these little wonders!

Rove beetles are another amazing creature. Some rove beetles can mimic ants and termites so well that they trick them into sharing their food supply. Their whole existence is dependent on how good a job they do at fooling their hosts. Remember that ants and termites are extremely territorial. They do not like intruders. When an intruder comes around, the ants will use their antennas to examine and check the feel and smell of the visitor. The mimicking that takes place has to be absolutely perfect or this species would die out. But, they do not die out. They fool them because God gave them the capacity to do so.

Why didn't He just design them to exist by some other means? Because He is a God of variety, He is a God that does things for His own good pleasure. He does it to amaze us and **SO THAT MEN ARE WITHOUT EXCUSE!** We cannot look at nature without seeing God's hand in every detail!

Clown beetles (HYSTERIDS) are an interesting group of beetles. They are not mimics, but they are designed to live with the ants, eat their food, and basically take every advantage of the ant's hospitality. Yet they do not look anything like ants, and they do not try to look like the ants. So why do the ants put up with them mooching their food and hanging out with them? It is because they have two small ports on the top of their head that secrete a liquid that makes the ants drunk. These beetles bring a little "joy and happiness" to the ants and in return the ants let them stay. I have to ask you, is this the result of natural processes over millions of years or is this the wonder of God displayed **SO THAT MEN ARE WITHOUT EXCUSE?** You cannot explain this with evolution! No way!

A word about antennae...

The antennae on beetles are fantastic. They are among the most highly designed in all of the insects. The antennae are equipped with incredibly sophisticated sensors that can detect food, find egg laying sights and detect changes in the atmosphere, including all kinds of environmental conditions such as temperature and humidity. Some beetles have specially designed little apparatuses to keep their antennae cleaned and groomed. Some beetles have sensory equipment to detect infrared radiation because they are drawn to smoldering branches after a fire. They can actually detect the heat. (They prefer their food barbecued.)

Male beetles may have very elaborate antenna structures to increase their powers of smell. Such adaptations are especially evident in species that use their power of smell to find a mate. The females release a hormone referred to as pheromones. The tiny pheromone molecules are released into the air and are diffused and diluted in the wind. Yet, the male beetle is capable of detecting a single pheromone molecule nearly a mile away, even if the female happens to be buried under all kinds of thick vegetation or sand. We spend millions of dollars trying to get the best possible sensitivity in the detection equipment we invent! So why can't we acknowledge and give credit to our Creator when we see such awesome design in these beetles? Speaking of incredible design and detection equipment, no discussion would be complete without mentioning Bloodhounds and many other dogs that are used to find missing persons, drugs, explosives and even detect cancer and other illnesses in people. These awesome animals, including the beetles, are a gift from God **SO THAT MEN ARE WITHOUT EXCUSE!**

Amazing examples of God's creativity…

There is another type of beetle, a type of rove beetle (STENUS) that does something amazing. When he panics and thinks he is being hunted, he has an interesting way of getting away. In the tip of his abdomen he has a gland that releases a liquid that lowers the surface tension of the water behind him. The increased surface tension of the water in front of him pulls him forward. He continues to rapidly pulse-release this chemical until he is able to literally ski across the water. The question I have is, "Why does he ski, when he could just fly away?" This is another example of God showing His creative design!

It is clear to me that God does not do things the easy way, but in a way that is more complex and mocks the idea of evolution which has no designer.

Certain Darkling beetles live in the hottest, most barren parts of the Namib Desert. These clever little beetles climb to the top of the sand dune and wait for the early morning fog to roll in from the sea. Their rear legs are extremely long, their middle legs are medium in length and their front legs are very short so that when fully extended they form a perfect angle by design. They lift up their hind end so when the fog comes rolling in and contacts their backs it condenses and rolls down special little troughs right to their mouths! Those troughs designed into their wing cases are textured in super-hydrophilic (extremely water-attracting) bumps as well as super-hydrophobic (water-repellent) valleys that together pull vapor out of the wind. **Accident? Happenstance? Luck? I don't think so!**

Our next example of special design often excites young people with comments like, "NO WAY!" Rhinoceros beetles are the world's strongest beetles. Some types can lift 850 times their own weight.

Another way to look at it would be a 200-pound man carrying 85 tons or this particular beetle carrying 8 cell phones! That is absolutely amazing!

ALL THIS, SO THAT MEN...

ARE WITHOUT EXCUSE!

How does the world's foremost and most famous evolutionist account for all this beautiful and spectacular design? Luck! That's correct - luck! (When did luck become a part of science?) Quoting Richard Dawkins, "The universe could so easily have remained lifeless, it is an astonishing <u>stroke of luck</u> that we are here."

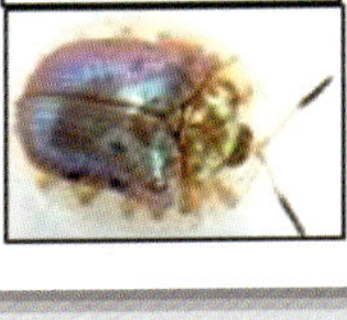

There are other families of beetles that are interesting to me because of their unusual behavior. Some Click beetles (ELATERIDAE) can catapult themselves 300 millimeters, which is 25 to 35 times their own length (like a six-foot man jumping 100 feet). Leaf-eating beetles are surefooted. There is a certain type of leaf-eating beetle that has awesome feet. Each one of his six feet has 5,000 little hairs that actually end with two bristles at the end of the hairs. So you actually have 10,000 of these bristles on each foot (mathematically 60,000 bristles) perfectly cut off flat at the bottom. Do you remember the scientific principle of surface tension? If you took two pieces of glass and wet them a little bit, and stuck them together you could not pull them apart. The surface tension becomes so strong it is like glue and you have to slide them apart. It is the same principle for these beetles. All those little hairs cut off perfectly flat secrete an oil film. The attraction is so strong, he could withstand a tornado and not let loose. If a predator tried to remove him or attack him, he could not be moved. Amazing!

Diving beetles like to go swimming. They dive underwater to catch their prey. To stay under the water, this beetle is able to trap an air bubble under its wing case. The trapped bubble acts just like a bottle of air on its back. Isn't that incredible? There is no way that could evolve or happen by accident!

Protection and defenses…

Beetles have a very hard armor coating and most of them have massive headgear and all kinds of horns, pinchers and mandibles. I think God designed these specifically to get young children's attention (and mine!).

For some of them, these attributes really aren't effective for protection, but are more for show and males wrestling for females (a guy thing☺). They would never have evolved. I believe they further showcase God's "creativity."

God made His creation so amazing and so unusual – with many characteristics that would never have evolved – so that man can clearly recognize the Creator in His work!

Other types of defenses or protection include: the use of illusion, mimicking, camouflage, and warning colors. There are beetles that mimic wasps and bees, not only in appearance but also in their flight patterns. It is absolutely amazing!

Some beetles mimic known poisonous bugs and insects so that potential predators will stay away or think twice.

Some of them use camouflage to look like tree bark or leaves or animal feces.

Some beetles use harmful chemicals that have to be stored in special chambers. They have to be able to fire on command and be accurate! Chemical compounds include: hydro-carbons, aldehydes, phenols, quinones, esters and acids including formic acid! There is one beetle, the clown beetle that actually stands on his head to fire his load. It is unbelievable!

Maybe you have heard of the Bombardier beetle. This beetle has something like a double-barreled shotgun: an appendage out of his rear section that he is able to blast chemicals out of.

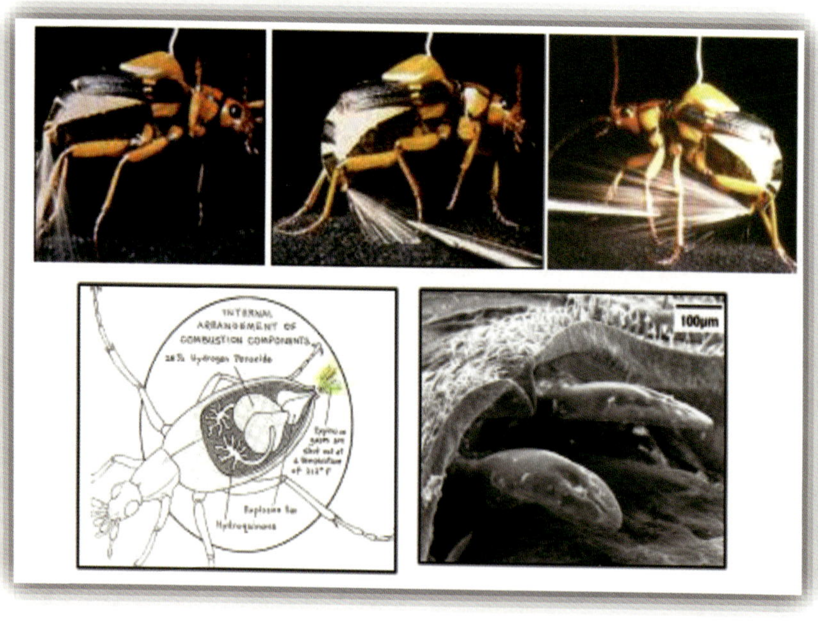

He can fire behind or tuck his "cannon" under his stomach to fire it forward – no need to turn his body around. It is perfectly movable. He fires out hot noxious gasses that are 212 degrees (boiling point plus)! Stop and think about it a minute; he has these two chemicals inside himself…hydrogen peroxide and hydro-quinone. They are stored in special chambers. When threatened, he must mix in a third chemical, which is the inhibitor and then load the mix into the pipes ready to fire. The third chemical was added so he doesn't blow himself up. Then at just the right moment, he adds a fourth chemical, an anti-inhibitor, so he can blast the enemy in the face! Bombadier beetles are being studied by NASA engineers to design new "pulsed" jet engines. Others are studying them to improve man's fuel injection systems in cars and drug delivery systems such as nebulizers.

How do you explain this? I'll tell you how to explain it… **we have an awesome God!**

For my last example, I want to talk about something that has fascinated me all my life. For fun, see if you can name what I am describing…

> "We are looking at an enzyme driven system, powered by a biological-chemical transporter. As a special chemical substance is energized, oxygen is pumped in to attach to individual carbon atoms. This stage kicks out an electron into a higher orbit. The oxygen and carbon are then released as carbon dioxide. As the electron drops back into its normal orbit, a bit of energy is released as a flash of light."

Is this some kind of new atomic invention? No, it's a simplified description of a firefly's light! When I was very young, we called them "lightening bugs" or "fireflies," but they are neither a bug nor a fly. They are – you guessed it – BEETLES!

God decided to give this little beetle its own tiny nuclear flashlight. This bioluminescent light system is nearly 100% efficient, cold light. Man's lighting is typically 10% efficient and the remainder is given off as heat.

Note: When it is your goal to provide light and not heat such as in a large office building in a hot southern climate, think of all the wasted energy consumed by air conditioning equipment to remove the heat. You get the picture? Man cannot duplicate what the firefly does, even in the most state-of-the-art laboratories. And that's not all! Quoting from a secular science paper from The Chicago Natural History Museum, entitled "Nature Magic,"

> "The firefly has another very great advantage. It can use the same fuel over and over. While the oxygen supply is shut off and the lamp is out, the burned material changes into fuel again. This is like being able to change ashes and cinders back into coal. No wonder lighting engineers wish they could discover the secret of the firefly's lamp, eight thousand times as efficient as an electric light bulb. The sort of light that only fireflies and a few other animals and plants can manufacture is the only

known light that isn't mainly heat. Man-made lights shine from burning up dead fuel, but this is living light."

Below is an optional quote for those who are eager for more scientific information… taken from the book, An Inordinate Fondness for Beetles by Arthur V. Evans and Charles L. Bellamy - pages 98 and 101.

"The details of bioluminescence in beetles are complex and not entirely understood. This enzyme system is powered by adenosine triphosphate, or ATP. An essential ingredient of all life forms, ATP functions as the biological transporter of chemical energy, providing the extra boost all cells need to perform their various tasks. Within the light-producing cells of the firefly, the enzyme luciferase attaches luciferin to ATP. This process energizes luciferin and allows oxygen that is pumped in through the trachea to attach to one of the carbon atoms of luciferin, kicking out an electron into higher orbit. The luciferin releases the oxygen and the carbon as carbon dioxide. As the electron drops back into its normal orbit, a bit of energy is released as a tiny flash of light. Multiply this activity by the thousands of cells found within the light-producing organ of a lampyrid and you have a flash of light that is easily visible to the human eye. This process

– the use of ATP and oxygen to produce light – is the exact opposite of the process by which plants capture the energy of the sun, photosynthesis."

A miniature nuclear flashlight in a structure smaller than a grain of rice... and you don't see the awesome design genius of our all-powerful and loving Creator and Savior?!

"For since the creation of the world God's invisible qualities—His eternal power and divine nature—have been clearly seen, being understood from what has been made, ***SO THAT MEN ARE WITHOUT EXCUSE!****" Romans 1:20*

Tortoise Beetles

I am going to conclude by telling a story...

One day there was a mouse crossing a wooden bridge with a herd of elephants. When they got to the other side, the mouse said to one of the elephants, "We really shook the heck out of that bridge didn't we?"

What a perfect illustration of the colossal pride and arrogance of man.

The bridge represents our journey through life. The herd of elephants represents God's direct and indirect providential care over the course of a lifetime. This care is displayed in the birth of a baby, the wonders in the heavens and the oceans, the miracle of the human body, and the unfathomable workings of nature and every creeping thing!

The mouse represents man at his best with all of his scientific methods, his medical breakthroughs, his technological discoveries.

He can rearrange things, often to his own detriment. He uses materials from the earth to build things, but gives no thanks to the One who put them there. So man struts across the bridge of life with the mammoth witness of God's power and design, gets to the other side - the end of his life, and declares, "I really shook that bridge."

Man makes nothing and he creates nothing without using materials from the earth that God created!

And from many of his efforts, he ends up with harmful synthetic materials, toxic waste and cancer-causing agents!

The mouse at least gave a little recognition to the elephants, but man and his pride rejects the Creator and Redeemer of our souls. What about you? Who do you credit for shaking the bridge? I have a secret for you, Jesus Christ not only shakes the bridge, **He is the only bridge** from death to life! Do you know Him? If you have not trusted Him, you need to trust Jesus Christ as your Lord and Savior. He is the one who made all of this wonderment. He is awesome!

A Note from the Author…

I'd like to share my concern with you after reading this little booklet. We can go through life and miss the design and diversity in the beetle world, ***but we must not miss the tremendous urgency of understanding and responding to Christ's death on the cross as payment for our sins!***

Two common attitudes that keep people from salvation are:

1. I'm okay, I'm not that bad; God will accept me as I am.
2. God will not send a "basically good" person to hell - the old argument that a loving and merciful God will not send sincere, well-meaning sinners to hell.

My friend, if you could live a life worthy of heaven (perfect), then Christ would have died for nothing. No person can be forgiven apart from Jesus Christ!

> ***"As it is written: There is no one righteous, not even one; there is no one who understands; no one who seeks God. All have turned away, they have together become worthless; there is no one who does good, not even one."***
>
> ***"Therefore no one will be declared righteous in God's sight by the works of the law; rather, through the law we become conscious of our sin."***
>
> ***-Romans 3:10-12, 20 (NIV)***

For it is by grace you have been saved, through faith—and this is not from yourselves, it is the gift of God - not by works, so that no one can boast. - Ephesians 2:8-9 (NIV)

If you believe that the love and mercy of God will insulate you from the penalty of hell, consider this, "Where was the love and mercy of God when His only Son was being brutally crucified?"

This question is difficult to answer because you do not comprehend the seriousness of your sin, and the unfathomable depth of God's love. In order to remain righteous - God must judge sin! In order for God to demonstrate His love, He must act! And act He did! God's solution was a substitutionary death. In other words, He paid our sin debt Himself. That is why trusting in Jesus is not optional, it is the only solution to our dilemma.

Expecting to enter heaven, without trusting that Jesus died on the cross in our place is like saying, "I believe Jesus died on the cross, but He did not have to die for me. I'm okay, I'm not that bad, God knows me…" Yes, God knows we are self-deluded, prideful sinners that are more interested in doing things our way than submitting to His Word. God tells us that we must accept Jesus as our Lord and Savior!

"Jesus answered, I am the way and the truth and the life. No one comes to the Father except through Me." John 14:6 (NIV)

"Salvation is found in no one else, for there is no other name under heaven given to mankind by which we must be saved." Acts 4:12 (NIV)

Salvation is as simple as ABC:

Agree with God that we are hell deserving sinners and turn from sin.

Believe that only trusting in the finished work of Jesus and asking Him to be your Savior is the answer.

Confess your decision for Christ with others as you live for Him and Praise His Name!

Published by:
Milk & Honey Ministries
Sunrise Christian Academy
5500 E. 45th Street N
Bel Aire, KS 67220
316-744-9262

If you liked this little booklet, you will find many more similar stories in my book, "HIGH Tech vs The HIGHEST Tech." Available also at Milk & Honey Ministries for $9.95.

Jeff & Team in Quito, Ecuador 2001
Building and Medical Mission Trip

"Riverdale Fellowship" - an outreach ministry founded at the Riverdale Marina, by Jeff and other Christian brothers in 2005

Three man team built home for the missionaries in the Amazon Jungle in 2001. Jeff with children from the Satta Maui Tribe.

Jeff in the Amazon Jungle with the Mission Team. Building a four room school house for Marubo Tribe in 2000.

Above: Jeff on a Medical & Evangelism Trip to Romania in 1994. The team visited mountain villages and orphanages.

Below: Jeff's next Trip to Romania in 1998
The team took in humanitarian aid for orphans.

1992 Bibles to Russia Mission Trip with Milk & Honey Ministries - Jeff with Russian Sailors & Children

Ministry in Canada – provides Jeff with **fond memories** of saints at Grace Bible Chapel, Strasbourg Bible Camp, Schumacher Public School, Timmins Trinity Christian School, Matheson Gospel Chapel and Cochron Gospel Chapel. (Locations in Moosejaw, Saskatchewan and Timmins, Ontario)

Jeff's ministry has blessed his life with **precious friends** from Camps, Churches, Schools, Jail/Bootcamp, Mission Trips, Recovery & Alternative Programs and Outreach. He is especially fond of young people. Jeff recalls one of his mentors, William MacDonald, teaching him a good lesson, "When feeding the flock, put the food down low where the lambs can get it, it won't hurt the sheep to bend over."

Jeff's Bio…

Jeff has been commended to the Lord's work for over 30 years and since 2007 by Woodside Bible Chapel in Maywood, IL. Jeff founded a ministry outreach in 2005 at the Riverdale Marina, called "Riverdale Fellowship" where he spoke every Sunday for 6 years until the Marina closed. He also serves as a chaplain for a Christian Motorcycle Club called, "Soldiers of Christ."

Jeff attended the Discipleship Intern Training Program (D.I.T.P.) in San Leandro, CA in 1985-86 where he had the privilege to study under Mr. William MacDonald, Jean Gibson, Carl Knott & Don Robertson.

Jeff spent 17 years as a full time minister at Oak Lawn Bible Chapel from 1987-2004. He has a real burden for evangelism and has been privileged to use his gifts throughout the United States and Canada. Jeff's interest in Missions has been greatly influenced by his mentor and friend Dr. Rob Lindsted. He has shared the love of Christ in Ecuador, Romania, Russia and Brazil (in the Amazon Jungle).

Jeff has also served for more than 25 years as an Auxiliary Chaplain in the Cook County Sheriff's Department Boot Camp and as in instructor in the "Life Learning Program" at the Cook County Jail. He also began a ministry in 2000 that he calls "Nature Talks" and has been preaching on this theme ever since.